COME, LORD JESUS

Devotionals
Compiled and Edited
by David Hazard

Come, Lord Jesus / Thomas à Kempis

A Day in Your Presence / Francis of Assisi

Early Will I Seek You / Augustine

I Promise You a Crown / Julian of Norwich

Majestic Is Your Name / Theresa of Avila

Mighty Is Your Hand / Andrew Murray

Safe Within Your Love / Hannah W. Smith

You Are My Hiding Place / Amy Carmichael

You Give Me New Life / Second-Century Disciples

You Set My Spirit Free / John of the Cross

Your Angels Guard My Steps / Bernard of Clairvaux

Thomas à Kempis

COME, LORD JESUS

Devotional Readings from
The Imitation of Christ

Edited for Today's Reader by
David Hazard

BETHANY HOUSE PUBLISHERS
MINNEAPOLIS, MINNESOTA 55438

Come, Lord Jesus
Copyright © 1999
David Hazard

Cover by Eric Walljasper

Published by Bethany House Publishers, 11400 Hampshire Ave. S. Minneapolis, Minnesota 55438, www.bethanyhouse.com

Library of Congress Cataloging-in-Publication Data

Imitatio Christi. English. Selections.
    Come, Lord Jesus : devotional readings from The imitation of Christ / Thomas a Kempis ; edited by David Hazard.
        p.   cm.
    ISBN 0–7642–2191–4 (pbk.)
    1. Meditations. I. Thomas, a Kempis, 1380–1471. II. Hazard, David. III. Title.
BV4821 .H39   1999   99–6568
242—dc21   CIP

DAVID HAZARD developed the REKINDLING THE INNER FIRE devotional series to encourage others to keep the "heart" of their faith alive and afire with love for God. He also feels a special need to help Christians of today to "meet" men and women of the past whose experience of God belongs to the whole church, for all the ages.

Hazard is an award-winning writer, the author of books for both adults and children, with international bestsellers among his many titles. He lives in northern Virginia with his wife, MaryLynne, and three children: Aaron, Joel, and Sarah Beth.

Contents

Introduction 9

1. "Follow me...." 19

2. The Spirit and the Word 23

3. Voice of Love 27

4. Our "Center" in God 31

5. The Upward Path 35

6. "You can defeat Satan...." 39

7. Satan's Foothold 43

8. Evil's Antidote 47

9. Why? 51

10. Judging 55

11. Useless Works 59

12. The Snare of Pleasure 63

13. The Snare of Envy 67

14. The Snare of Unbelief 71

15. Spiritual Armor 75

16. "You can defeat the flesh...." 79
17. Benefit of Adversity 83
18. Self-Reliance 87
19. Attachments 91
20. Vain Knowledge 95
21. Customs of Men........................ 99
22. Resisting God's Word 103
23. Reason 107
24. Under Authority 109
25. Strength of My Life 113
26. "You can defeat the world...." 117
27. Worldly Desires 121
28. Worldly People.......................... 125
29. Worldly Wisdom 129
30. Trusting People 133
31. The Faults of Others 137
32. Dependence on "the World" 141
33. Habits 145
34. God Directs All Things 149
35. A Little "Sweetness" 153
36. "Imitate Jesus...." 157
37. Await the Promises 159
38. "My child, trust in me...." 163
39. Accept Me, Father 169
40. Journey's End 171

Introduction

*O*n a summer day in 1392, a young boy hammered on the door of a small house in Deventer, in the north European lowlands. Would he be accepted into the religious community that lived here? He felt a passion for God. He did not want to go back home to the sweaty work of an apprentice blacksmith at his father's forge. What would he do if these Christian brothers said *no*?

As he waited for someone to answer, he couldn't have known that more than his personal future hung in the balance. This was an important day for Christian history, and for Western literature, too.

The old prior who opened the wooden door looked down at the boy—dark, healthy-looking, shy, wearing clogs and rough-spun clothes—and listened incredulously to his stammered explanation. *He can only be twelve or thirteen. Why would a young boy want to pursue the toughness of a religious life?*

Nonetheless, something in the boy's sincere and steady gaze, something in the intensity of his desire—"*I want to seek God*"—was very convincing. The door swung wider to let him enter . . . and soon the hearts of these Augustinian brothers also opened to receive among them this unlikely boy, whose name would echo through history and around the globe . . . known to us today as Thomas à Kempis.

Had he been turned away, the world would never have been given one of its most beloved spiritual classics, *The Imitation of Christ*.

It is ironic—but also fitting—that *The Imitation of Christ* is arguably the best-known and best-loved volume in Christian literature (or world literature, for that matter), yet so little is known about its author. Thomas's virtual anonymity stands as testimony that the man who penned this phenomenal work had truly grasped the utter humility of the One about whom he wrote.

About *The Imitation of Christ* itself: Next to the Bible, probably no other spiritual work has been so widely read or had so much influence. Many millions have turned to it for renewal, guidance, comfort, conviction. No matter what any of us comes looking for, when we open its pages we discover something greater than what we were seeking—and that is *an encounter with the living Spirit of Jesus Christ . . . like a living flame in the soul's depths.*

The Imitation of Christ gains its reputation (be warned) for its uncanny power to steer the soul into the living presence of Christ. And—as I say, fittingly—it's in the light of the Savior's real presence that Thomas à Kempis all but disappears.

Still, what little is known of the man raises alluring questions.

Of Thomas's early life, we know that he was born in 1379 or '80 in the village of Kempen, where his father smithed. Haemerken ("little hammer") was a well-earned surname. His older brother became prior at the monastery of Mount St. Agnes, near Zwolle. Was it his father's passion for shaping metal that spoke to Thomas, calling him to shape men's souls in the spiritual image of Jesus? Not a scrap of diary, not a private letter remains, to tell us how the boy sensed that his soul was a cold wick, longing to be ignited by Christ.

Several years after being accepted at the community in Deventer, probably in 1406, Thomas took the vows of poverty, chastity, and obedience. Life in a religious community was not an "escape" from the world—not by a long stretch: The world in Thomas's day was a crazy man on a furious horse galloping toward disaster.

Historian Barbara Tuchman has referred to the time in which Thomas lived as "the calamitous fourteenth century" with very good reason. The Black Plague came in wave after wave. Not a single feudal lord in his castle, not a peasant in his country croft, nor a village burgher in his walled town, was safe. You woke to find your wife, husband, child, or parent with eyes rolled back and fixed and tongue lolling purple-black. This horror would wipe out more than a third of Europe.

Not only did men's hearts melt within them, souls were shaken, too. The church—and therefore the foundation of Western civilization—was crumbling as one religio-political earthquake after another shook the landscape. Popes fled for their lives as one anti-pope after another fought for Peter's chair. A legitimate pope would no sooner regain power than a king or an emperor would attack his authority. The common man and woman walked fearfully into the cathedral sanctuary of a Sunday morning—not so much afraid of facing God with a stained heart as fearing that some new political or religious sociopath would have sent an edict that demanded they swear allegiance or be burned alive. If the plague did not kill your body, some maniac wanted your soul.

And among the Christian brother- and sisterhoods, monastic life was gasping. Bernard of Clairvaux's revival of the twelfth century, and Francis of Assisi's of the early fourteenth, had flared and dulled. Dissension, petty bickering, and the constant effort to curry favor with some duke or king colored religious life. Heads of monasteries were sometimes little more than political toadies. And so to say the body of Christ on earth was sick is an understatement.

The community Thomas joined was not, however, an officially recognized "order." It was more a set of related "houses" and part of a grassroots movement known as "the modern devotion." Its single, simple characteristic was that its followers were determined to imitate the simple life of Jesus and his first disciples. They lived, prayed, sang, worked together, and shared everything—therefore, choosing for themselves the name Brothers of the Common Life.

The spirit within Thomas began to take shape. There was a profound respect for all men and women. A sense that God was—despite earthly tragedy and human mess—invisibly governing all things. A *presence* within him . . . majestic but humble, strong and beautiful. His spiritual eyes and ears were opened . . . and his heart was taken captive.

He felt desperate, pushed from within, to describe what cannot be seen with human eyes—and to tell other people how to know Him.

Idyllic as Thomas's life might sound, his community was soon on dangerously thin ice with the official church. They promoted learning and taught without charge—"for the love of God." They also worked outside the community, and so they were dependent on no one for their livelihood. It was this—their independence—that made the Brothers distrusted by bishops and nobles alike. (If you don't control someone's wallet or their conscience, how do you know where their loyalties lie?)

We can concede that Thomas was probably youthful and idealistic—but what was it that helped such a young man transcend the social order of his day and remain loyal to a suspect, counter-cultural religious group? It seems Thomas obeyed instincts that told him, *When the world is in terror and chaos, you have to push the world aside and find a spiritual rock to stand on.*

Soon the world's turmoil would rattle the peace of these communal houses.

As the movement's founder, Gerard Groote, lay dying, he knew the revival would dissipate without some form. He chose the ancient Rule of St. Augustine as the governing structure for his scattered houses— and it was those vows that Thomas recited, and this Order that guided him into the priesthood in 1413.

If his life's calling was now a settled issue, his personal safety was not.

There was a church dispute over which bishop would take charge of the episcopal see of Utrecht, in which district Thomas's house lay. One group made their nomination . . . which the Pope, Martin V, ignored after discovering the man was illiterate—and plain stupid besides. He placed his own man, who could not be manipulated by the locals, in authority.

With an unusual degree of democratic fervor, the

people refused to accept him. It's characteristic today to believe that "bucking the system" is probably always right. In this case, it was an example of the attitude we so often see destroying the body of Christ today: *If the church doesn't do things our way, let's seize power and do things our way.*

The humility of Christ is always lost to those who are determined to fight for their rights.

The Pope slammed them with an interdict: *No sacraments, no Mass, until you obey.* This was grave indeed; the next step was to be declared a heretic.

When Thomas's Order sided with the Pope, they had to flee for their safety. It made no difference the years they had quietly, gently served and taught these people. If they didn't escape there could be blood in the streets. Their blood.

Thomas's brother, now elderly and ill, became even sicker during the hasty and rough evacuation ordered by the superiors. For months he suffered, and finally died.

And now more questions about Thomas come to the surface:

You would think that seeing the dark underside of the church and the vicious nature of humanity would have made Thomas cynical or bitter. Sure, people talk pious Christian-talk—as long as they get what they want. But when things don't go their way, self-interest takes over. . . . Like swine, they can trample anyone who denies their demands. Isn't this what sours many people today?—the fact that when you scratch through their veneer of Christian "manners," even Christian people get ugly?

The spiritual light that shone in Thomas only grew stronger. Until the end of his life, in July 1471, he continued to face physical and spiritual dangers most of us never see. What was the secret of his inner resilience? What did he know about living in the presence of Christ—and allowing Christ to live in him—that you and I need to know?

Those spiritual "secrets" are revealed on the pages that follow. Too many modern Christians have found Thomas's antique language a problem, and for that reason I've updated the language and sentence structure while remaining faithful to his concepts . . . even (and especially) the challenging ones. Other readers have failed to benefit fully from *The Imitation* because they don't understand terms or spiritual practices that Thomas mentions, and which were in common use in his day. These are explained in simple terms, so you can get the greatest benefit from this spiritual masterwork.

When all was done, I arranged Thomas à Kempis's words and thoughts into a forty-day devotional journey. Its aim is to help rekindle in you a true spiritual faith by opening the eyes and ears of your soul to the living presence of Christ—which, of course, was Thomas's single goal.

My prayer is that you *will* meet Jesus in the quiet sanctuary of your soul . . . and carry Him into the traffic and noise and challenge of today's world . . . *with* you and *in* you . . . so the world may hear the voice and know the graceful beauty of our living Lord.

David Hazard
June 1999

1

"Follow me. . . ."

*T*he true light that gives light to every man [has come]
into the world.

John 1:9

"*I* am the light of the world," says Christ, our Lord.
"Whoever follows me will never walk in darkness, but
will have the light of life" (John 8:12).

Christ has called us to follow Him, walking in the
kind of spiritual light that leads us on the path of
eternal life.

By asking us to follow Him, He means:

First, that we should follow His teachings—
believing that God is our Father and trusting Him to
care for us, learning to overcome the world and the

devil, serving others who are also children of the Father.

Second, that we should adopt His attitudes—that the Father knows what is best for us and we should humbly surrender ourselves to His will and direction, that of the Father, willing to battle against evil and temptation, acting in charity for all.

So, as we understand His doctrines, and by imitating His character, spiritual light dawns within our souls. We live in the light, and the light comes to live in us. With our inner vision renewed, we begin to see life, and the world, and ourselves, from God's point of view. And because we perceive reality differently, we begin to act differently, too.

This is how we experience deliverance from spiritual darkness and come to "walk in the light, as he is in the light" (1 John 1:7).

Let Christ's innermost attitudes fill you, then, and you will understand this path of deliverance from blindness and struggle.

"Study" Christ in this way:

Consider how He placed all His trust in God, and not in men, so His soul was standing firm on God alone. Trust in the Father alone was the rock on which Jesus' soul stood. And so He was not cast down with disappointment at the evil and failures of men.

Consider how He lived simply, possessing little, giving thanks to God, and receiving everything as a good gift from His hands. Because He did not count possessions as His "right," because He did not measure His worth in terms of worldly possessions, He was free inside to enjoy much, or enjoy little. So worldly goods did not have control over Him.

Consider how He focused on the eternal goodness and beauty of God, so that His heart was attached to God by a longing for the unseen beauties of eternity. So real and wonderful was the realm of heaven to Him, that the world and its temptations paled and held little attraction.

This is what I mean when I tell you to meditate on Christ, I mean the life that was in Him. This will teach you how to adjust your own attitudes. And when you change the inner man, approaching life as our Lord approached it, you will make incredible gains in spiritual virtue and strength. . . .

The man or woman who practices this kind of meditation will know what it means to have the eye of the soul opened and to begin to "see" God. He or she will perceive the heart of the gospel and know what it means to have Christ actually dwelling within by faith.

If you do what I am telling you, you understand why it is said that Christ is the "hidden manna" and the "bread of life." And your soul will experience deep satisfaction, here in the hungry wasteland of this world, where so many are starving within.

Father, I ask you to lead me on a new path in spirit, deeper into you.

I want to learn how to imitate the heart attitudes of your Son, Jesus, who came to show me how to open my soul to you. . . .

Open the eyes of my soul to perceive your unseen glory, beauty, truth, holiness. Open my ears to hear your voice.

Today, Father, I ask you to walk in the depths of my being and begin a deeper work . . . until all the motives and attitudes that govern me . . . are governed only by you.

2
The Spirit and the Word

The letter [of the law without the Spirit] kills, but the Spirit gives life.

2 Corinthians 3: 6 [editor's note]

*M*any who hear the Gospels preached, nevertheless, do not taste the goodness of God in their soul. Why is this so?

Because they do not adopt the spirit of Christ as they listen to the Word. That is, they do not listen as children, accepting the Word with simple faith.

Instead, they let their *skepticism* get in the way, saying to God in their hearts, *I'll believe what you say if you prove it to me.* Or they let their secret *unbelief* get in the way, thinking, *I have never experienced these things, so they can't be true.* Or they analyze and criticize Scripture with the intellect, until the theological workings of their mind have killed the life that is in the Word.

Do you want to understand the Word of Life that is in the Gospels? Then conform your spirit to Christ's as nearly as you can. Accept that the Word is true, and act on it as if you believe it with all your heart—and when any voice in your soul begins to whisper against the Word, command it to be silent.

If we hear the Word and do not act on it—that is, act on it in faith, as Christ would—then it is fruitless, and we are wasting our time (see James 1:22).

But, you may object, isn't it enough to learn the teachings of the Word?

No, you must instruct the heart, too. For what good does it do to be able to explain the mysteries of the Trinity if you lack the humble, surrendered heart of Christ and fail to live under the daily guidance of the Trinity? All that knowledge in your head would be a waste of time.

All our reasoning abilities amount to nothing, even if we search out theological complexities. Why?

Because reason does not create in you a heart that perceives God, so that you are caught up in His holiness and beauty. Only then do you forsake all other pursuits, so your heart is "separated" from the world, and you live a simple, clean, and holy life.

It is living this kind of life, with your heart attached to the heart of God, that pleases Him ... as Christ pleased the Father ... and makes you know you are His own. In this way, the Word comes alive to you, and in you. ...

Father, reveal my own heart to me as I hear your holy Word.

Show me the hardened attitudes that keep the Word from burying itself deep in my soul. ... Show me my doubt ... unbelief ... bitterness over "unanswered" prayer ... jealousy toward others who seem "more blessed" ... and my resistance to your claim on my life as Creator.

Create in me the heart of a child, who acts in simple faith and learns his father's words are right and true.

Father, I want to move beyond mere knowledge of doctrine ... and encounter you in the very depths of my being.

3
Voice of Love

*"You diligently study the Scriptures because you think
that by them you possess eternal life. These are the
Scriptures that testify about me, yet you refuse
to come to me to have life."*

John 5:39–40

*I*f we want to be like Christ, our Lord, we will seek
God in His Word.

But as I've told you, we are not to be like those who
knew every jot and tittle of the Scriptures but could not
see our Lord for who He was ... though He was
standing right in front of them, *the Word made flesh*!

When you open God's Word, you are seeking the
voice of Love, which is pure and selfless in its
overflowing charity. You should take the openhearted

attitude of Christ. We do not read the Word only to search it for truth . . . we read the Word to let it search us, to show us the truth about ourselves. Again, we do not read the Word to learn how to direct God in what He should be doing—we read it to accept direction in how we must live.

So we must read all of Scripture, even the parts that are difficult to read, or seem harsh. Do not read only the beautiful poetic parts that seem "nice" or agreeable to you. For you limit the power of the Word.

Some Christians make a grave mistake along these lines. They read books by well-educated men and accept what they claim because they respect the authority of those writing. But they come as skeptics to the Word of God and question the credibility of those God inspired to write it.

The same is true when they read the writings of spiritual masters and the fathers of the church—they think, *Maybe these people were religious fanatics. Should I trust what they say?* Or else the writer is obviously simple and unlearned, and they think, *This is too spiritual and simplistic. It doesn't take into account the complexity of life, the way sophisticated, secular writings do.*

I tell you, beware of this "sophisticated" attitude,

which leaves the soul in full control, accepting what it will and will not obey.

Pay little attention to the "position" or "sophisticated style" of the one writing—whatever you read. Instead, *pay attention to its effect on your soul.* Do the words speak to your inner man with truth that directs you to greater purity? More simplicity? More faithfulness and love? . . . Take care to act on the truth, and you will know the transforming power of the words.

For who are we to force the Word of God to submit to us? We are hardly a breath in time. We are blades of grass that rise with the dawn and then are gone with the heat of a single day.

But the Word of God—and what it brings to life in our soul—will stand firm forever.

Father, deep in me is the continuing urge to resist you and your authority over me.

I say that I want to grow in spirit . . . but I want growth on my terms.

You tell me to pray, and I think, I will if you show me how to get the answers I want.

You tell me to forgive, and I think, I will if it makes sense to forgive. *You tell me, "It is forbidden to . . ." and I think,* But it's okay for me.

Teach me to read your Word faithfully, and not as a rebel. Teach me to hear your voice of love . . . trusting that everything you tell me is for my good.

4
Our "Center" in God

All my longings lie open before you, O Lord; my sighing is not hidden from you.

Psalm 38:9

We are restless in our souls. We look for something to fill us, trying this, running after that. When we become intolerably bored, we seek distraction by meddling in other people's lives and affairs.

There is a way to escape these surging shallows of the soul and move out into the ocean of peace that is in God. That is by learning how to gather together all your restless energies and center them in God . . . until He directs you in a single, passionate focus.

Throughout the ages, men and women have learned how to focus their fires of the spirit through the art of contemplation. They have done so by learning to still themselves before God, patiently watching over their souls to see what restless thoughts and desires came to pull it away from its peace. Once they saw these desires for what they were—voices of the world, nagging them to come and find their value in contentment, in pursuits that pass away with time—they knew their soul's enemies. And so from their solid place of peace and quiet in God's presence, they could say to these voices, firmly, "No."

This is what it means to put to death the untamed desires and surges of the flesh by the power of the Spirit (see Romans 8:13). It is what the saints have called "mortification." The reason we need to practice mortification of our uncontrolled energies is to free and focus us, with all the power of unified being, in the direction and purpose for which God created us. In this way, we come to serve God with our whole mind, body, and spirit.

Because so few practice contemplation like this, we see many Christians who are weak, unfocused, and easily distracted by the many voices of the world. They can hardly resist even one vice. They can hardly raise enough energy or interest to serve the Lord even in the smallest ways, because they cannot see how simple, unnoticed service will be of personal benefit.

And beneath it all, they wonder why their heart is not as kindled with the fire of devotion to the Lord as it is passionate to chase after worldly hobbies, accomplishments, and belongings. They wonder why their heart is cold toward God—and it is because contemplation has not opened the eye of the inner man to see Him ... to see *in* Him ... all the holiness ... beauty ... truth ... love ... that has ever existed. For the poor flickers of these qualities in us are only sparks from His heart, where they have burned from all eternity.

But I tell you this: If you fix the eyes of your soul on Him, in holy contemplation of His deep mysteries and wonders, the fire that is in Him will begin to purge your soul of its taste for the dead pulp of worldly things. It will create in you a taste for heavenly things.

And you will begin to experience, in the center of your being, the serene strength and peace of heaven— the peace you are really longing for.

Father, I ask you to teach me. Help me to see that I can gently push away the voices that call and distract me . . . demanding from me until I am empty, burned out . . . left without any passion or caring.

Cause me to still my soul right now . . . and to fix my inner being on the vision of you . . . passionate . . . holy . . . afire with love.

5
The Upward Path

Stand in awe [of God] . . . commune with your own heart . . . and be still.

Psalm 4:4 KJV [editor's note]

*P*erhaps you have experienced times when you were more spiritually minded than other times. Maybe you felt great passion for God when you were converted—or in your youth, when you felt excitement for all of life.

But now it is different. Now you notice that your spiritual ambitions flare up . . . and in a short time grow cool.

There are three things that dampen the fires of our spiritual passion: the world, the devil, and our own flesh. The soul is under constant assault from these three quarters.

I am writing to show you the way to ignite the passion of your soul and to keep it alive, by drawing near to the "living fire," which is God himself. And the way I will show you is the upward path, which is to take on the heart of Jesus Christ, who came to show us this path into the flaming heart of God (John 14:6) where our fire for life and goodness can never be put out.

You will remember that I spoke to you about putting to death the influences that call to your flesh, by the practice of contemplation ... by focusing your mind and soul on the deep heart of God. This is a simple practice, very freeing to the soul, and I strongly recommend that you cultivate this as a spiritual discipline you practice every day.

The busy person, and even Christians who know little about the workings of the soul, may look at you and think you are accomplishing nothing. To these people, contemplation is idle, fruitless, a luxury. They have no idea that contemplation is the very beginning of all true works done by the Spirit in us ... the first turn of the key that unlocks our imprisoned souls so we are free to serve God with vision and power.

Why is this so? Because while we are in this fallen state, we are subject to all manner of evil and self-centered inclinations. We say we love God. We say we want to do what's right and serve God. But until we are free in spirit, we cannot help ourselves. We are weak, and chained to our own will. When it comes right down to it, in our hearts we tell God, *I want my way. And I don't think the things I want are that wrong. I'll serve you in certain ways. . . . I'll offer you money so other people can do your work . . . but don't pressure me to do anything I don't want to do.*

It is this very thing that must be broken—the evil inclination to live apart from God, living according to our own plans and dictates, while we offer God tokens.

Do you see it? It is your will, the hidden source of energy that powers all you say and do that must be converted—so the fire that drives you from within is His fire. On the upward path I will show you, you and I may become one with Him, united in spirit.

And so I tell you, learn to identify quickly that self-will that inclines you toward independence from God . . . and from there leads you on the path down toward a world of evils, great and small. As you learn how to choose this upward path every day—and many times in a day!—you will see how quickly the virtues of Christ begin to appear in you.

I know it is hard in the beginning to leave selfish and evil habits, harder to allow the Spirit to break you of demanding your own will . . . and surrendering to Him. But it is even harder to find, in the end, that you have followed a path of your own choosing, and seen—too late, in agony—that you have led yourself away from the eternal joy of heaven.

Father, I cannot surrender my will to you on my own. Many have tried and become miserable legalists—joyless, loveless, unhealthy people who are unable to freely love, freely live, freely serve.

Today, Father, by your Spirit, open my eyes to one person, one event, that challenges my self-will . . . so I can see myself clearly. Give me the power of your grace to respond, instead, in the love and strength of Christ.

Only if you teach me, Father, can I begin to learn the life of Christ in me.

6

"You can defeat Satan. . . ."

The darkness is passing and the true light is already shining. . . . I write to you . . . because you have overcome the evil one.

1 John 2:8, 13

"My child," says the Lord. . . .

"You are in greater danger than you know. For in the world, which lies in the lap of the wicked one, you are subject to *confusion*. And this is the greatest tool of your enemy, Satan.

"So many desires and passions pull at you. So many thoughts and ideas cross your mind. And you think,

Maybe this is a good thing—it seems to be right for me, and it's what I think I want.

"Sometimes you may believe you're sensing the Holy Spirit, telling you what's right and good for you. But not every thought—no matter how good it seems—comes from my Spirit. Or you may think you're sensing the true desires of your own heart. But it may surprise you to know that not every desire you feel originates in you.

"What I am telling you is this: It is hard for any man or woman to judge whether it is a good or an evil spirit that is influencing his or her heart, guiding to do one thing or another. Many people are deceived into thinking my Holy Spirit is guiding them . . . and in the end they are defeated and brought down . . . and so they are discouraged and blame Me . . . when Satan has led them astray through whisperings and desirings. . . .

"You can defeat Satan. And I will tell you how.

"Knowing your blindness . . . knowing you can be easily confused . . . come before Me in humility, and pray:

"*My* Father, this is the thought I am thinking . . . and this is what my heart seems to want. But I don't know if this is a good desire . . . if it is given to me by you, Lord, or by the Enemy.

Only you, Father, know what's best for me. Only you are powerful enough, wise enough, to guide me in what is right and good. I can't see my own way, and I can't walk in the path of goodness unless you lead me.

Give me only what I need to do your will. Give me as much or as little as you will. Supply my need whenever you choose, and not according to my demands. . . . Because I know that you will lead me on the path that brings best profit to my soul—whether I am given the desires of my heart or my desires are withheld. . . .

Only you, Father, know how to guide me to the place where your life and light are strong in me . . . giving me the interior life I truly need and desire . . . and making your presence strong in me so others see your invisible radiance in me. . . .

For I know that the highest purpose of my life is to have the light and peace of your presence in me . . . giving me strength to overcome Satan and the world . . . and allowing your life to be in me . . . so others are drawn to the light. . . ."

7

Satan's Foothold

*Reverently fear and worship the Lord, and turn
[entirely] away from evil.*

Proverbs 3:7 AMP [editor's note]

*O*ur life on earth is warfare. What Christ offers us
is peace, and a way to overcome the spirits that war
against us—if we follow Him.

On our way to victory, we will benefit if we also
learn to practice *vigilance*—that is, the discipline of
keeping watch over our own soul in prayer. Like a
guard on a fortress wall, I say, keep a sharp eye out for
the place, people, and things that tempt you. For
behind them lies your soul's great enemy.

Satan, our enemy, never rests. He waits in quiet. He
comes in pleasant guise. That is why we need to be

alert, so that he will not sneak up on us or deceive us. . . .

And do not be fooled by thinking you are beyond temptation. No one is so holy he cannot be tempted, and no place is so safe that the Evil One cannot find you. As long as we are in the body we are subject to temptation . . . for it is the flesh itself that hungers for the things forbidden. If we are not drawn by one temptation, we are pulled by another. This is the state we are in, since we lost our first innocence.

Many people try to escape temptation merely by staying away from the people and places that tempt them. This is admirable and helps for a time. But in the end those who run away from temptation will fail. Why? It is because they use the wrong strategy. You cannot run from temptation. And if you fail to face the truth about the unsatisfied hunger in you, you leave Satan a foothold.

The only thing to do to defeat evil, is this: Stand your ground when temptation comes. Turn your face to the Lord and humbly surrender yourself to Him, saying, "Look at the evil desire that is in me. If you do not show me how to fill my hunger with *something good*, I will fall to this temptation. Help me. Show me the way of escape, and I will do whatever you say."

Then patiently *do* what the Lord shows you to do. He will help you. And you will find that evil loses its grip as you seek after what is good.

A man or woman can run away from outward occasions for sin. But if they do not deal with the hungers that gnaw at them from within, they will never even begin to win in the battle of spirit and flesh. And they will always be subject to the wiles of the evil one.

Father, I need you to help me face the truth about the hungers that lie in my heart. I've become so good at letting other people see I'm a "good person" that I'm not even honest with myself about the true desires of my heart.

For every want that's in me, show me your way to fill it. Feed my soul, Father, so I will not allow the Evil One to tempt me with his sweet offerings.

8

Evil's Antidote

"Our Father . . . deliver us from evil."

Matthew 6:9, 13 KJV

---

*For you, O Lord, have delivered my soul from death . . .
my feet from stumbling, that I may walk before the Lord
in the land of the living.*

Psalm 116:8–9

The Enemy is easily defeated, if we resist him and shut him out of the heart—the way you bar the gate on an invading enemy. . . .

One way that we are easily defeated is to despair when we are tempted. When we despair, we look at ourselves, and say, "Look at me. I'm so hopeless." That is a mistake, because *our hope is not in ourselves, it is in the Lord!*

A second mistake is to give up the battle when we have only lost the first small skirmish. By that I mean, we may catch ourselves entertaining a tempting thought . . . and give in wholeheartedly, thinking, *I've given in this far. I might as well go the rest of the way.*

Let's say an impure thought comes to mind—not one of us can help this from happening. The difference is this: You can turn aside from it and fix your eyes on the Lord—or you can dwell on the thought and develop it into a full image in your mind. Then you begin to direct the fantasy until it gives you the satisfaction you desire . . . until the day comes when the evil images are so rooted in you that you act on them, and they are not fantasy but sin born out of the corruption in your heart.

Isn't this the way it goes?

And so the Enemy gains his foothold little by little, till he has full entrance in you. Because you did not resist him at the very beginning. The more lax you are, failing to put him out immediately, the more ground he gains in you, inch by inch. And every day he becomes a little stronger, more sure about winning the victory over your soul.

Do not be like the person who waits too long to take strong medicine, until a sickness has taken hold of their body . . . and the help is too late. Turn to the Lord, place all your hope in Him, the moment you are tempted. The vision of His goodness and strength will make you strong to resist the Enemy.

This is the best known antidote for temptation and sin.

Father, the truth is . . . I'm so proud that I think I can toy with evil and not be harmed by it. I think I can enjoy the good feeling it gives me and my soul will not be harmed.

When it would feel good to gossip about the flaws of another person . . . to bend the truth to protect myself . . . to take "just a little" . . . to toy with "harmless" fantasies. Open my eyes and show me how sickness is spreading in my soul.

Father, help me today to find my hope—my soul-healing from sin—in you.

9
Why?

And we pray this in order that you may [grow] in the knowledge of God [that comes from intimate encounters with His might], being strengthened with all power according to his glorious might so that you may have great endurance and patience. . . .

Colossians 1:10–11 [editor's note]

*M*any Christians wonder: Why does God allow us to be tempted at all? Or why let temptation continue throughout our lives—why not just deliver us totally from the desires that become twisted and wrong and lead us into sin?

For some, temptation is greatest at the beginning of their conversion. For others, it is far greater the longer they have been Christians. Some are troubled with certain temptations all their lives, while others are barely stirred by the wisp of an evil thought.

God is not the author of evil, sin, or temptation, yet in His divine providence He ordains things in this way. Why He does so—allowing some to wrestle with sin and others to easily live good lives—is a mystery that lies deep in His own heart. We only know that He chooses the path that will lead each one of His children to the greatest strength in spirit, the deepest experience of His Spirit's saving might.

This much we can say for sure: When we feel ourselves weakening, we may cast our souls on the mercy and strength of God. And in His infinite love, from the fatherly pity in His heart, it will please Him to draw our souls to himself and take care of our every need. And at the same time, He will go before us in power and grace to defeat the overwhelming odds against us. For He will always rescue those who come to Him and admit they are powerless.

This, too, we know: How a man or woman responds when they are tempted proves where they stand in faith. For some blithely run to sin, and say, "God will forgive me anyway." Others resist sin and secretly become self-righteous, forgetting it is only the Lord's strength that makes them strong.

And others run to the Lord, showing their simple trust in Him. By this we show that we have gained ground, following Christ on the way that leads us to oneness with God.

Father, if facing my weaknesses drives me closer to you—so I can know your mercy and your incredible strength—I will trust in your wisdom. Thank you for every tether that keeps my soul nearer to you.

10
Judging

"I am merciful," declares the Lord. . . .

Jeremiah 3:12

I will show you one point on the path where Satan is able to trip up most Christians. Some, in fact, fall into a deep pit and never recover.

I am referring to the sin of judging others.

We should be growing in our ability to judge our own heart—that is, in the ability to weigh our motives carefully. But we should be growing, equally, in our restraint when it comes to judging other people.

When we learn how to let God search and sift our hearts, we profit greatly in spirit. For He shows us how we use boasts to impress others when we are feeling small and insecure and desperate to seem better than we are. He shows us how we use anger, flattery, or tears, to manipulate when we want to get our way.

But when we judge others, our efforts are totally in vain. Why? Because we are not God, and so we cannot really know the heart of another. Nor do we know how God plans to work in that person's life, possibly even using their weakness or sin to break them and turn them to himself. We judge foolishly, because we do not see the end of God's dealings yet. In our limited judgment, we will write off someone as "useless," "lazy," "stubborn," "evil," or "beyond hope." And so we close ourselves off from being vessels of God's grace and mercy to that one. This is wrong.

We will never be able to judge as God judges—and remember, His judgment will only come at the end of all things. Our judgment is full of the worm holes of self-love. His is pure. We judge by ourselves. He judges by love.

When we judge—let us be honest—the reason is this: someone has crossed our will, or violated our standards. So we are angry, or disgusted, and in an attempt to appease our own troubled soul we pronounce judgment. *Guilty. To the devil with him.*

And the enemy has triumphed because he has

tricked us into sitting in the seat of judgment, which belongs to God. And just like him, we fall into the deep pit of pride.

Father, deliver me from the sin of presumption and pride.

If I begin to judge someone who is weak, stubborn, calloused, mean, manipulative—drive me to my knees instead, and give me the wisdom and charity to pray for their soul— and for mine.

11

Useless Works

"When you give to the needy, do not announce it with trumpets, as the hypocrites do . . . to be honored by men. I tell you the truth, they have received their reward in full . . . do not let your left hand know what your right hand is doing, so that your giving may be in secret . . . your Father, who sees what is done in secret, will reward you."

Matthew 6:2–4

There is another trap in which our enemy catches the soul of the Christian. This is the trap of useless "good works."

Some people do their good deeds so that they can be noticed by the "right people." Or they offer help and favors to those in high positions, or the wealthy. Their hope, of course, is that their good work will gain them some praise, favor, position, or a reputation ... and truly that is all the reward they will ever get. And all the while they think they are so spiritual, they are in deception, making no progress in Christ.

For God who looks on the heart knows when a task is done out of self-love, and not in selfless charity for His sake.

But when we do act with kindness, patience, or self-giving, imitating Christ our Lord, we begin to make great gains in overcoming the devil and our own soul. The smallest act of selfless love, however silly it might seem to the world, is pleasing to God. For then we are acting in His character, and it pleases Him to see His sons and daughters reflecting even the tiniest flicker of His image in this dark, selfish world.

Keep this in mind: If we love God much, it is nothing to give much. Whoever does even the smallest deed well, does a great thing. And the one who acts for the good of all—even though it costs him dearly—does a very great thing.

Charity—the pure, selfless love of God—does not seek anything for itself in its acts. It wants only to bring praise and glory to God. . . . When you feel the smallest spark of charity in you, you should be overjoyed. For you are escaping another snare of the devil, who is always whispering to us that our only reward and gain come here on earth. In this way, he leaves many earthbound and helpless to move on in soul to God.

Father, so often I want my "goodness" to be seen by other people, so they'll know what a good person I am.

Today, direct me to one selfless act I can do—one small, unnoticed favor or courtesy—that I can do in secret and in your name. Let a small glimmer of your brightness shine into this world today through my life.

12

The Snare of Pleasure

But mark this: There will be terrible times in the last days. People will be . . . lovers of pleasure rather than lovers of God. . . . Have nothing to do with them.

2 Timothy 3:1–2, 4

Do not think your soul is secure and immovable—not as long as you are in this life. Haven't you ever known a man or woman who seems good and spiritual—and then seen them fall away from God?

The person who thinks they will never fall suffers even greater damage when they slip. *You remain humble, and depend on God for every moment of your soul's safety and strength*. Only in this humble spirit do you stand a chance of avoiding the snares of the Evil One.

And here is a hidden snare you must avoid:

Many Christians allow themselves to daydream about pleasures they know are forbidden. They think, *I'm not acting on these thoughts. So what does it hurt?* They are already many steps down the road, deep in enemy territory.

Before you know it, Satan has mesmerized you, using your own appetites. He has led you out of your fantasies into real indulgence. He has stirred your flesh, and your senses have moved you out of the realm of the spirit and into the world where you are left to grub out a few moments of pleasure. But what you desire is a shiny illusion, dangled before your eyes. In the end, you do not experience the inner delight you thought sin would give you. In fact, you are empty and cold within, slinking back home with guilt and remorse. You have burned your conscience and shattered the peace of your soul.

It is often said: "A few moments of happiness tonight—a heartful of ache and sorrow in the morning."

So it is—with empty illusions that promise

satisfaction—Satan hypnotizes and leads astray. So it is he leads us out from the presence, safety, and fulfillment that is in God—out to where his dark forces can gnaw on our soul with the teeth of regret, bitterness, and sorrow.

Father, keep me alert to the voice that whispers inside, "What does it matter if you indulge these thoughts?" Let me see through the shiny illusions—and see the snare that lies beyond.

Teach me, Father, how to let you give me what my soul really needs to live: respect . . . acceptance . . . integrity . . . love . . . a "home" in your heart.

Keep me from following after evil.

13

The Snare of Envy

A heart at peace gives life to the body, but envy rots the bones.

Proverbs 14:30

The most miserable person on earth is the man or woman who does not know how to turn to God—or how to draw from God all that the soul needs to live. They are easily disturbed, easily driven to fear and anxiety, easily driven to self-pity and dissatisfaction.

Why are these people so easily troubled?

It is because they cannot control circumstances or get life to turn out exactly the way they want it to. Also, because they cannot have exactly what they want. They're constantly looking at others, thinking, *Look at him. He's had all the advantages. But I have to work so hard, and I don't get the rewards. It's not fair.* Or, *She's so gifted. So talented. Everyone just loves her. Why did God not bless me in that way?*

Well, I would love to meet these "specially blessed" people who have "so many advantages" you don't have. Where are they? Show me one.

No one who lives in this world can avoid hardship, loss, trouble, sickness, or heartache. Not even a king or the pope himself.

I'll tell you the source of your trouble. You imagine that a perfect someone else learned how to find more "favor" with God than you do—or that God chooses certain "favorites," while He mistreats or ignores others. The whole basis of your thinking is wrong because you equate worldly comforts—health, money, good looks, great opportunities—with spiritual blessing.

The one who is most favored by God is one who has been taught by the Spirit how to bear all things with patience and joy, for the sake of knowing God better. This man or woman is powerful in spirit, and they overcome every hardship or loss with grace, strength, and brilliance from within. They have favor with God because they are humble and easy for Him to direct, so

He can quickly show them how to turn their suffering and loss into victory.

If you want to stay weak in spirit, caught in a snare of envy that rips your soul apart, then keep praying as you're praying: *Look at so-and-so. He has everything—wealth, power, position, people admire him—and on top of all that, he's great looking. How is that fair, God?*

But if you want to escape Satan's trap, then fix the eyes of your soul on the goodness of God himself, as He orders all things . . . and who gives eternal rewards that do not decay and crumble like these earthly things you value so much. Only in the light of eternal things will you be able to see reality as it is—to see that the things you are tempted to envy will fail, and soon pass away.

Father, it's so easy for me to envy someone who seems to have "everything"—or to think you've treated me unfairly when someone has been given advantages I don't have.

Help me to take my eyes off other people—their possessions, position, power, or looks. By your Spirit, open my eyes to see your amazing wisdom . . . to know and accept the path you've chosen for me . . . even if it leads through pain, loss, impairment, and being ignored by others.

Only let me know your living presence with me . . . and that will be enough.

14
The Snare of Unbelief

"*Since we are God's offspring, we should not think
that [God] is like gold or silver or stone—an image
made by man's design and skill. In the past God
overlooked such ignorance, but now he commands all
people everywhere to repent.*"

Acts 17:29–30 [editor's note]

If you want real interior strength, and a robust
soul, then you must learn what it means to "fear" the
Lord.

It has been written, "The fear of the Lord is the
beginning of knowledge" (Proverbs 1:7). But do you

know what this means? The writer is not telling us to have a craven, quaking fear of the Lord, so that we are afraid *of* Him or afraid to *approach* Him. Rather, he is telling us to open the eyes of our soul, and to see the Lord as He is—mighty and sovereign over all things, with a power that no other power can equal. He is telling us to have such intense belief and respect for the awesome power of God that we see how little, puny, and futile all other "powers" are by comparison. When we fear—or respect—the amazing power of God in this way, we will not put our trust or dependency in anything else.

When we recognize how vast are His goodness and power, we will not want to be out from under His direction. We will see that being "free from God" to do "whatever we want" is actually the worst thing for us— because then we are out on our own, where other powers can influence and lead us in the direction of our soul's destruction and death.

Therefore, learn to recognize the voices that tell you: *Forget this talk about "submitting to God" and letting Him direct your steps. Do this thing . . . follow this path . . . give in to this desire . . . and it will give you what God cannot give you.*

This is the trap of unbelief . . . and many fall into it, though they believe right Christian doctrines in their head. It is unbelief because they trust in something that is created—an "idol"—while they say they trust the Creator.

Ask God, then, to give you *compunction* in heart—which is the stab of anguish you need to feel the moment you are turning away from God and placing your trust in other things. It is the shock of waking up to find yourself headed down the wrong road, and the urgency to get back to the right way. We need this reminder whenever we are being tempted to place more trust in wealth, possessions, or any person . . . than in God's awesome might.

You can be sure Satan doesn't want you to feel any compunction. He wants to dull your heart, so you don't see anything wrong with trusting in everything *but* God. This is the condition many find themselves in. They don't see how far they are away, in exile, from the heavenly country where their soul may dwell now—knowing the strength of complete peace they can have—*if* they will utterly trust God for all things.

*F*ather, so many voices call me—to trust in money for security; to trust in friends for acceptance; to trust in accomplishments, possessions, or position for my worth.

Now, in this quiet moment, I ask you to lift the eyes of my soul—so I may "see" your awesome power. Help me to see through things that have only the appearance of power.

Renew my inner vision of your might and provision—so that I learn to trust in you—and in nothing else.

15
Spiritual Armor

Let us . . . put on the armor of light.

———

Romans 13:12

I have shown you some of the ways Satan traps good souls who are walking the path to the kingdom of God. There are many other ways, as well.

Do you want to arm yourself like a knight in battle, so you will be safe from his attacks? Then put on the armor of the spiritual warrior, which is the *humility* and *charity* of Christ.

What is humility? It is the attitude of heart that says, *You are sovereign, O God, and you are only good. My peace and strength come from submitting only to you, no matter what kind of difficult circumstances or people you allow to enter my life.*

Humility keeps us from worrying about ourselves and our rights and gives us the strength that comes from abandoning ourselves to the care of God.

And what is charity? It is the ability to see God at work in the lives of all people. To understand that He calls us to act in meekness, kindness, gentleness, patience, and respect for all—knowing that these attitudes allow the Spirit to work through us. For as we forget about ourselves, and stop worrying about how others make us feel, we become vessels of God's life in us. Then it is possible for His love to flow through us. Others will see this shining virtue in us, and it will eventually bring forth spiritual fruit in their lives, too. For—don't forget—we are surrounded by people who are under attack from the Evil One, as well.

If you take on this "armor," you will surely defeat all the evil advances of the Enemy—whether they are attacks against your own soul or against other people. . . .

If you want to wear this, the "armor" of Christ, I recommend you set aside time every day and do this:

Ask the Spirit to search your heart . . . to shine His light deep . . . to show you where your self-will and insistence on having your own way is still strong. As

He shows us—and He will!—surrender those demands to God.

Then, ask the Spirit to search your heart again . . . to show you where your judgment is limiting the grace and charity of God toward someone.

This practice of *examining your soul before God, in the light of His presence*, will always help you, in this our fight against the devil.

Father, examine my heart and show me where I am agreeing with the Evil One.

Every time I say, "Haven't I given up enough? Haven't I struggled enough? Don't I deserve this?"—show me how I'm giving in to the temptation to consider something "mine by right." And give me your humility.

Every time I say, "He doesn't deserve help or forgiveness," show me that I'm giving in to the temptation to sit in your seat of judgment. And give me your charity.

16

"You can defeat the flesh. . . ."

You were bought at a price. Therefore honor God with your body.

1 Corinthians 6:20

Therefore . . . we have an obligation—but it is not to the sinful nature [that dwells in our flesh]. . . .

Romans 8:12 [editor's note]

It is not always right to say that our struggle is with Satan. Often our troubles come from our own flesh.

In referring to the *flesh*, I mean both our physical

body and our tendency to place other people in the place of God.

In our struggle with the physical body, we wrestle against all the hungers of our being—such as gluttony and sensuality. These appetites overpower some immediately. But more often they simply hold us in a dull sort of bondage, so we keep giving in to our drives in unhealthy and disordered ways. Soon, food or drink or sexuality gains the upper hand, and we have to have more to satisfy us ... while we find less and less pleasure.

In our tendency to place people before God, we think that other human beings can fill our deepest desires. And, of course, they cannot. Yet sometimes we are almost literally slaves to others—sometimes trying to please them, at other times angry and demanding of them to give us what we want. All the while we hope this little "false god" will be able to give us exactly what we need. Over and over, we are disappointed when it cannot.

This is why we teach that our affections can become disordered. That is, they are set upon the wrong one— because we are trying to settle the deepest needs of our soul by drawing on another limited human being instead of learning to go to God.

If you want to be free in spirit, you must learn to master the flesh—and this is a battle indeed.

You can defeat the flesh. But in this great effort, you will need all the assistance of the Holy Spirit. For no one can win this, the place of *self-mastery*, without God's help.

Call on Him, then. Lay open your carnal appetites, and show Him all your weaknesses. Do not fear, do not hide in your shame—trust in His mercy and strength. And pray:

Father, give me the inner power of your grace. Help me to overcome by relying on your Spirit to feed me. Without this, I cannot overcome the temptations of my physical body . . . or the temptation to seek what I need in someone else.

You know me well, Father—how weak I am! You know how quickly I give in to my self and my appetites. You know how easily a little adversity makes me feel the need to pamper my flesh and take refuge in my "comforts."

I know that if I do not fight this battle, I will never gain mastery over my self . . . and will always be subject to the drives of the flesh. But if I learn . . . slowly . . . painstakingly . . . to lean on you as we gain the upper hand in this, you will crown my efforts—with true freedom.

17

Benefit of Adversity

How gracious [the Lord] will be when you cry for help! . . . Although the Lord gives you the bread of adversity and the water of affliction, your teachers will be hidden no more; with [the eyes of the soul] you will see them.

———

Isaiah 30:19–20 [editor's note]

It is a good thing to go through hard times, and even to experience grief and loss. Of course it doesn't seem like a good thing to our flesh.

But adversity makes us realize that this world is not our true home, for here we have no lasting peace or comfort. The hard times remind us that we are exiles in a hostile place. Loss reminds us not to seek our ultimate security or well-being in any created thing. For everything here is subject to change and death.

It is also a good thing to experience times when people speak evil of us or think poorly of us. It's good to have others oppose our will and contradict our words. Again, none of this seems good to the flesh.

When people attack our reputation—when they ignore us or treat us as fools, with scorn, it teaches us to turn to God for our worth and approval. And so we learn another lesson in surrendering ourselves, in humility, only to God . . . and to no one else. For we are of great worth to Him (see Matthew 6:26), though others may despise and misuse us.

In fact, many Christians have learned to accept adversity and mistreatment by others with great joy. How can this be? Is there something wrong with these people? No, they recognize that such opposition to their spirit defends them from pride—that ever-present force in our soul that secretly demands we be treated like little kings or gods. They recognize that when others speak evil of them or belittle them, they are driven to God to find their worth in Him . . . and His judgment of our worth is infinitely more valuable than the value any creature can place on us.

The secret of finding benefit in adversity is simple:

Whenever troubles or opposition come, turn immediately to God. Ask Him to teach you whatever He will in the circumstance. Ask Him to train your spirit to listen only for His word of approval.

In doing this, your soul becomes strong and firm because it is learning to stand only on the One who is our rock and fortress (Psalm 18:2). And, in this way, the soul becomes unshakable, fixed and firm . . . standing strong in God alone.

Father, unless I know your love and presence, I will never be strong when circumstances—or people—are against me.

Teach me in some small way today how to benefit in spirit from adversity.

18
Self-Reliance

"All men are like grass, and all their glory is like the flowers of the field. . . . The grass withers and the flowers fall, but the word of our God stands forever."

———

Isaiah 40:6, 8

Some men and women pride themselves on being self-reliant. They are proud of their capabilities—and secretly think, *I don't need to depend on anyone to help me. I can do very well on my own.* In their hearts, they think that a person who relies on others—even on the Lord— is weak.

Do not trust in yourself. For this will always lead you off on the path of your own choosing. And though you will accomplish many things, you will be apart from God.

Instead, place all your trust in God. Do everything you can to respond to His grace, so that your life is more fitted to His plans each day. And you will be pleased to find that He forms your will around His own, so that you find great fulfillment in accomplishing the goals He has in mind.

Do not trust in your own wisdom. For you and I are limited creatures—we do not have the higher perspective God has, since He has been alive from all eternity, and sees all hearts, and His Spirit is present everywhere. Can't you see how foolish it is to put all your trust in your own "intuition" or "experience"— since you are a small, created being?

Instead, place your trust in this: Each day, God's Spirit will issue in graces, like an outflowing river. And these graces—of wisdom, insight, guidance, conviction, empowerment—will guide you in the path He wants you to walk every day. The grace of God will shed light on your errors and sins until you see how foolish it is to live life under your own "guidance" and will enable you to humbly follow God's leadership.

Be careful—especially if you are a person of means—not to let money go to your head. And do not feel secure just because you have wealthy friends.

Many have trusted in the power of money, only to watch it slip through their fingers like dust . . . or found themselves stricken with an illness or loss that no amount of money can help.

See that you don't put your trust in your physical body, either its strength or its good looks. For illness and age come to us all, and the body fails us in the end.

Let your honor and achievement be in this: *To have the glory of the living God—the Light of Life!—fill you.* As you learn to rest your soul in Him—trusting Him to care for you, letting Him love others through you—you will know in the depths of your being what it means to draw your life from God . . . and to have an eternal rock to rely upon.

Father, I really prefer to rely on myself . . . on what I can do . . . what I can have.

I say that my self-reliance is a good thing, so I don't put demands on others. But, in fact, I want my way! And I don't like being disappointed.

Teach me, Father, how to rest all my demands and desires in you . . . and to let you transform them into the desire to be strong in you. For you alone are eternal.

19
Attachments

*[Do not love] the approval and the praise and the glory
that come from men . . . more than the glory
that comes from God.*

John 12:43 AMP [editor's note]

Do not let your heart become overly attached to
people. They cannot give you what your heart longs for.
Love people, but let your relationships be held in an
open hand.

You see, every one of us forms attachments to those
we think will benefit us most—whether because of their
light spirit or worldly interests or financial strength. We
rarely seek a relationship that will challenge us in spirit.
And in the end, we remain inside a circle of
acquaintances who only reinforce our choices and our

personality—and this does not lead to growth and transformation in the character of Christ.

So then, I want you to seek out men and women with spiritual wisdom and insight. People who will be discreet, so you can open your soul to them and discuss your needs and weaknesses. People whom you can trust because they have a passionate reverence for God, because they live and move in His powerful presence.

And as for the company you keep—choose friends who are humble and simple in spirit, who are devoted to God, and whose lives demonstrate that they really believe what they say they believe. When you get together, avoid dirty and vain talk, but rather encourage each other to live godly lives.

If you are a man, be very, very cautious about friendships with women. Likewise, if you are a woman, be careful about friendships with men. It's too easy to become confused and wind up where you should not be!

Most of all, seek God's company early in the morning, as soon as you wake. Go throughout the day knowing that your unseen Friend is beside you, encouraging you by His Spirit, allowing His ministering angels to guide your steps and protect you.

Learn to know His movements in the depths of your soul . . . so that little by little you become attached to Him before all others. This is how you come to love God with all your heart, mind, soul, and strength (see Matthew 22:37–40).

In the end, because you form this first bond of loyalty to God, you will gain the distance and objectivity you need to be a true friend to other people. You will come to love them with a charity that wants what is best for them.

If we do not love in this order—loving God first— we are not free or healthy enough in ourselves. Our needs and demands get in the way, and we are only fooling ourselves to say we love other people.

Father, I see that my "love" for other people is most often only self-love. I love them when they make me feel a certain way or give me what I want—when they don't irritate me too much!

In this quiet moment, I set my eyes on you—Love itself— who came down from heaven to live among us—and to die for us.

Show me, today, some of my self-centered "loves." Begin to free me from attachments that keep me from growing in spirit.

93

20
Vain Knowledge

"*The wisdom of the [worldly] wise will perish, the intelligence of the intelligent will vanish.*"

Isaiah 29:14 [editor's note]

I want to know Christ . . . becoming like him. . . .

Philippians 3:10

*E*very man and woman has a measure of curiosity and the desire to learn. Feeling that we *know* makes us feel wise and secure.

But learning—apart from the wisdom of God—is limited indeed. . . .

Even so, learning makes us feel we have a place of

respect among other people. And some make it a habit to let others know right away. They are always mentioning their accomplishments or the schools where they have studied. And most of us love to offer our opinions—and love it even more when someone is "awed" at our great insight.

You cannot live in this world without knowledge and learning. But there is a great deal of knowledge that is of little benefit to the soul.

The kind of knowledge that will really profit you—in soul as well as in body—is the knowledge that comes as you learn how to walk with God in the humble character of Christ. That is, the intimate knowledge that comes as your spirit interacts with Christ's Spirit, and He begins to shine and become present in you. This means more than talking about the Scriptures or discussing doctrine: Words do not feed the soul . . . but letting your spirit come to know Christ by this kind of contact with His Spirit, works a kind of spiritual wisdom into the fiber of your being. It changes you from the heart, so you understand why it is right to surrender your life to God . . . and ultimately leads you to live a good, clean life, with a clear conscience.

Yes, worldly knowledge is necessary. But the

spiritual knowledge that comes from imitating Christ's Spirit will make you stable and strong in God.

And if your worldly learning has made you proud, so that you think you do not need this knowledge of Christ, I must tell you—you are in great darkness and serious danger. . . .

Father, I thank you for the gift of a good mind and many interests. Yet I want to "learn" Christ most of all.

Today I ask that you stir me with your Spirit when someone pushes me in the wrong way . . . and help me to surrender my irritation to you . . . receiving the kindness and patience I need to reply as Christ would.

I give my being to you, so that I may know you and so that your life is lived through me.

21

Customs of Men

The customs of the people are vain.

Jeremiah 10:3 KJV

*I*t is a hard thing, when you choose to follow Christ, to break away from the customs of this world. I am speaking not only of the ways of worldly culture, but also the customs that govern men and women in how they behave.

For instance, it is considered manly to strike back when another man strikes you or to respond with strong words when another man insults you. If you do not respond this way, other men will call you weak. And it is considered customary among women to talk secretly about others when they are not around. And if you fail to enter into this gossip, they might begin to gossip about you.

Yes, worldly custom is the means by which we measure if someone is "like us"—whether or not we are comfortable with them and accept them. We know that others are measuring us, too, by whether or not we do what they do. And because we are afraid others will think we are strange, and reject us, we give in and act just like them.

Why do you want to be conformed to the image of others? Is it *that* important to be liked by them? In conforming to their image, you lose yourself . . . and you surely lose your way in God.

If you want to become a true, mature man or woman, you must learn how to overcome the world and to break free from the gravity of its evil and backbiting. You must learn how to stand in Christ for what you believe. And in this He will help you.

When you feel yourself being pulled into a conversation or some action that is low and mean—*resist*. Ask the Lord to help you escape little evils you have been accustomed to.

This is how the Holy Spirit begins to give you inner strength, little by little. And if you take these small steps, you will soon make great strides toward becoming a person who is free—not pushed or influenced by the pressure of others.

Father, it is so easy to slide into the customs and habits of other people . . . so easy to want to "fit in."

Will you help me today, Lord, to act and to speak—or to be silent—as love requires, so that I am less like other people and more like you?

22

Resisting God's Word

[*"When the Word of God falls on a resistant heart it is like the seed] that fell on rocky places . . . he lasts only a short time. . . . But the one who received the seed that fell on good soil . . . produces a [good] crop."*

Matthew 13:20–21, 23 [editor's note]

---

*W*hen you read the Holy Scriptures, you should read them to see what you can learn about God's love and charity for all.

Some read or listen to the Scriptures only to learn what rules they must keep. Or they read so they can explain the complexities of doctrine and the mysteries about God. Some love the poetic passages or the sublime wisdom they find there. . . .

It is almighty God who speaks to us in Scripture, and what is He trying to tell us except that *we are to become like Him in love?*

For God is always trying to speak to our hearts through the Law, which He gave in love to free us from heathen darkness—through wisdom, which gives us His eternal perspective and brings peace to our hearts.

Yet our flesh can keep us from hearing the living voice of the Spirit behind the Scriptures.

First, our human reason interrupts: *God cannot really mean for me to do this . . . or to believe this.*

Or our corrupted conscience feels uncomfortable: *God cannot really mean for me to be that perfect.*

Or the cool intellect takes over and merely compares and criticizes the Word of God . . . as if God is happy to have us critique His commands and thoughts!

If you want to gain anything from the Scriptures, open your heart and submit to the Word! Do not sit above it, deciding whether or not it is to your liking. Sit beneath the Word, and let it search out all the willful, obstinate ways that are in you . . . and let it direct you as you surrender yourself to God to walk in His ways.

*F*ather, I want your Word to direct my steps. But if your Spirit and your grace do not help me overcome my stubborn resistance, I will only "appreciate" your Word and not let it go deep inside.

Father, I want your Word to become the living seed of new and eternal life in me. Open the hardened places of my heart to receive it.

23

Reason

What is faith? It is the confident assurance . . . even though we cannot see. . . .

Hebrews 11:1 TLB

I will tell you right now: you may find it easy to avoid excesses of the flesh. And perhaps you've even learned to control your tongue and not say everything that comes to mind.

But there is one stronghold of the flesh: it is our *ability to reason*. I must explain.

Reason is our ability to look at events and gather facts and form an opinion. This is how we gain knowledge of the world and how we base our decisions.

But reason and human intelligence cannot perceive

God or understand His ways. This kind of understanding begins with *faith*—that is, when we accept truths about God that He has revealed to us, truths that cannot be "proven" by reason, intellect, or science. So our reasoning abilities will never lead us to God.

Reason is not evil, it is a gift of God. But our kind of human knowledge is limited and does not lead to the radiant light of truth that shines into this dark world to reveal God to us.

So it is that we must learn a new way of knowing—that is, the walk of faith. This is exactly where our flesh recoils. Because faith does not seem reasonable to the mind of man, dependent as it is on "observations" and "facts."

O Truth that is God . . . speak to my soul!

Father, I want to still myself now . . . and let the light of your eternal reality dawn in me.

Let me know something of your real presence . . . here . . . now.

24
Under Authority

I urge . . . that requests, prayers, intercession and thanksgiving be made for everyone—for . . . all those in authority, that we may live peaceful and quiet lives. . . .

1 Timothy 2:1–2

*I*t is greatly freeing when you learn how to live at rest under authority. There are few who learn how to do this or even understand its importance in building a healthy spirit.

Men and women seek total freedom. They do not like it when someone is over them telling them what to do. When they have to take direction or follow someone's leadership, they are in turmoil. They complain and grumble. They think that in their quiet rebellion they are exerting "independence"—but they do not see the real truth.

The truth is that all authority is placed over us by God. But, of course, in order to really believe that, you have to believe in God's sovereignty and the fact that nothing happens by chance—it is all of His design. Then you have to be willing to rest under His authority, allowing Him to make the choices that lie in His will for you.

It is this ability that will give rest to your soul—to see God as ruler over all and to trust that all His choices for us are working some good in our lives. For then, just like Christ, our lives are surrendered to Him and hidden in His will.

Go wherever you want to. Make your own choices. Pick the leader you are willing to follow. Choose which counsel you will accept and which you will disregard. But you will never be at rest within—and you will never be free.

For there is no prison so great as the prison of a man's own will, which has not been broken and surrendered to the good sovereignty of God.

Father, when it comes down to it, I don't want to trust you completely. I think I know what's best for me— what I need and when I need it.

Show me the heights and depths of your goodness and greatness so that I am convinced my soul's only rest and purpose are found in you.

25
Strength of My Life

I know that nothing good lives in me, that is, in my sinful nature. [But] if the Spirit of [God] . . . is living in you, he . . . will also give [his] life to your mortal bodies through his Spirit. . . .

Romans 7:18; 8:11 [editor's note]

*I*t is a great piece of revelation when you realize that your flesh is very weak.

Consider: There is no goodness in us that did not come from God. If there is any holiness in us, it is only because God moved upon us and drew us to himself first. And if God were to withdraw His hand of mercy, none of it would stand. We would fall and be broken in our sin. Because it is He who keeps our soul.

Do you think you have wisdom or knowledge? You

were given a good mind—and all wisdom comes down from the Father. Do you think you are strong in body? In spirit? If the Lord did not strengthen your inner being with His invisible hand, you would collapse.

On our own, we cannot defend ourselves—not from Satan or any earthly enemy or any evil word spoken against us. All protection comes from the Father. We may try to live sexually pure lives, but if the Lord did not guard our mind and body, we would fall to animal lusts.

Yes, if the Lord did not hold the very atoms of our body together, we would perish and be blown away like dust.

But . . . if the Lord comes to us with even a little of His outpouring grace to strengthen, life courses through us and our spirits soar like eagles. If we have felt out of sorts, shaken, or unstable, a mere brush of His Spirit makes us firm and strong again. If we have been cold, nearly dead in soul, the flames of His passing will rekindle holy love within us.

Do you understand what I am getting at? You should not count on the flesh at all. For it is perishing a little more every day. And the only strengths you have are gifts from God.

That is why I have been telling you to put no confidence in the flesh.

Father, I thank you that every good thing, every ability I have, is a gift from you. Forgive me for imagining I did something to deserve it.

I know that without you I can do nothing. And I know that when you call me to follow you—to serve you even in some difficult task—you will give me grace and strength so that nothing will be impossible.

26

"You can defeat the world. . . ."

"Him who overcomes I will make a pillar in the temple of my God."

Revelation 3:12

"My child," says the Lord. . . .

"You experience misery in the world—loss, betrayal, struggle, defeat. And I know the sadness and turmoil you feel.

"For I descended from heaven not because I was forced to but out of my intense love for you. I came so that I could experience every hardship the fallen world puts you through, so I could fully understand your sorrows.

"Yes, I came as the Son of Man so that you could follow me and learn the way to patiently walk through the turmoil of life. It does no good to resist or complain, because terrible things happen to all sons and daughters of men. And so I came to show you how to bear up and overcome every misery by having a spirit that is strong, brilliant, and alive forevermore.

"Yes, you can defeat the turmoil of this world. And I will tell you how.

"You must begin by fixing the eye of your soul on me. For from the hour I was born until the moment I died, I was never without some sorrow or lack. I was born into lowly circumstances. When I left home I owned nothing but the clothes on my back. Men spoke against me, behind my back. The men in power called me 'demon possessed' and plotted against my life. They constantly tried to trap me into saying or doing something for which they could declare me guilty.

"I spoke to their soul's pain and emptiness; they repaid me with slander. I performed miracles of healing and deliverance and set souls free from the bondage of sin; they blasphemed me. I taught them the way to escape the crushing weight of the Law and how to

118

know God as their own true Father; they contradicted and 'corrected' me. . . .

"Keep your eye on me at all times and, from within, you will begin to experience the grace that gives patience—the same grace that was in me. This is the beginning point of all the strength I mean to give you, if you listen to all I am about to tell you. . . ."

Lord, you showed such amazing patience against such opposition in this world. And you bore all things, trusting yourself fully to the good will of the Father—no matter what circumstances were against you.

If you—the Son of God—struggled as you did, what makes me think I should be spared hardship in this life? I need to walk closely with you and learn the inner strength that gave you such power in spirit . . . power to accept and fulfill the will of the Father, no matter what came against you.

Teach me—by means of my struggles—how to rely on you and walk in the way that leads to the freedom in spirit that overcomes the world.

27
Worldly Desires

Everything in the world—the cravings of sinful man, the lust of his eyes, and the boasting of what he has and does—comes not from the Father but from the world. The world and its desires pass away, but the man who does the will of God lives forever.

1 John 2:16–17

Do you wonder how it is that some have such strength, such sublime dignity—even a kind of light shining from within—in the face of tremendous struggle?

These are men and women, great in the faith, who have learned the secret of setting the eyes of the soul on Christ. While others look with the physical eye and see only their immediate surroundings, these have

121

practiced the spiritual discipline of contemplation—by which our inner man is trained to see through the visible into the invisible.

This was their secret: through contemplation they gained a view of the invisible realm. Soon they understood what it meant to have their citizenship there instead of here. They comprehended the truth that we are eternal beings, and in only a short time these bodies will die but our spirits will live forever— to be later reunited with our resurrected bodies. So they saw the temporary nature of all created things and realized how foolish it is to spend all the energies of the spirit to get wealth, possessions, houses, and land. How foolish to wrap our affections around another created being, whose life will pass like our own.

Learning to view life this way, learning to hold temporary things in an open hand, it became easier and easier for them to put to death—or "mortify"—the desires that pull at the flesh. For once you've caught sight of the eternal wonders that lie above us and seen the slow decay of all that lies around us, it is far easier to keep worldly desires from consuming you.

And so they became free in the inner man and able

to focus all their energy in the path on which God directed them.

Isn't this what you want—freedom from the grip of transitory things that captivate your heart? Freedom from the drive to have more . . . and more?

Father, there are many things in this world that consume my energies . . . capture my soul.

I want to know how to rule over my own spirit so I am a slave to no created thing: no person, no possession, no position, no image I've created of my self.

In this quiet moment, I ask you to still my thoughts, to open my mind to a vision of your eternal realm so my soul can rise to you and see the truth about this passing world.

28
Worldly People

All man's efforts [are for nothing], his appetite [for the things of this world] is never satisfied.

Ecclesiastes 6:7 [editor's note]

*T*his world is full of people who have little use for religion or any kind of spirituality. They believe that this world is most likely all there is, and so they are intent on getting everything they can out of this life— owning, doing, trying everything. The only limits are their appetites.

Run from people like these.

The more you focus on the world, the more enamored of it you become. And the more you fall in love with material things and a life of sophistication, the less attention you will pay to things of the spirit. For the love of the world quenches the soul's fire for God. It doesn't matter that you set out with good intentions or tell yourself "It won't happen to me," the world's attraction is deceiving. The more you pursue the good things it has to offer, the more you tell yourself "Christianity is stuffy and confining. This is what I want—freedom, enjoyment."

What we don't see is that the world and its pleasures are taking us captive. Soon we are slaves, working every day to pay for the good things we need ... working to keep pace with worldly friends so we can impress them with what we own and where we've traveled.

I am not saying these people are not pleasant. Their company is enjoyable, and they always have some interesting story to tell, a new experience to talk about.

But I can tell you from experience, the more you get involved with worldly people, the more you take up their attitudes, and the more you think, *What am I doing following the narrow path of Christ? Maybe I need to go out and just enjoy living.* There are many times I should have paid attention to what was going on in my own soul while I was with worldly people—because by listening to their attitudes, I set myself up for battles with envy and the desire for worldly living later. . . .

It is urgent that you keep watch over your soul, for in this life it will always want to pull away from God and seek its life elsewhere.

Father, Keeper of my Soul! I ask that you shepherd me through this world.

Keep me alert when someone's impressive life, accomplishments, possessions, or travels, make me start to think that serving you is a waste of time. Keep me awake to my own desires, so I can be honest about them with you.

Keep me close to you.

29
Worldly Wisdom

With humility comes [true] wisdom.

Proverbs 11:2 [editor's note]

*H*ave you ever noticed that those who have worldly wisdom also have an attitude of superiority?

Oh, they may seem pleasant enough on the surface. But eventually the various degrees of arrogance begin to show through. Some let it come out in conversation, in which they can't help but mention their education and degrees, their accomplishments, or their skill in business. Some seem genuinely meek at first, but then the stubborn independence comes out. They will not be told anything by anybody because their view is the *right* one.

What deceives these people is this: worldly wisdom

gives the individual competence and mastery and builds his sense of importance. It allows you not only to take charge of circumstances but to direct people who are less competent and knowledgeable. You begin to think that you are *over* them and that you are *worth more* than they are because of what you know.

These people never see that their soul has fallen into the trap of *arrogance*. The only "final opinion" they seek is their own because they believe that their own ability to understand is superior to that of others around them. Why take direction from anyone else?—that would put you *beneath* them. And they cannot bear to think they are less than someone else.

A man or woman is very unwise if they allow worldly wisdom to lead them into the deadly sin of pride. They are very far from the beginning of the true path to God—which is humility, the first spiritual virtue of Christ himself (see Philippians 2). And all their knowledge will never benefit the soul. . . .

I warn you: do not think you are above others because of your wisdom or skills. So you are a little more knowledgeable than someone else—what is that? Your good mind and your natural abilities were *given to you* by God. That should make your heart stand in awe of God and make you grateful.

Yes, every ability you have is a gift. You did not attain it because you are better than someone else. Therefore, stop comparing yourself to other people—whether you are "better than" or "not as good as" they are.

Father, I compare myself to other people all the time, and it's become so "normal" I hardly notice that I do it. Thank you for showing me the trap this is.

I thank you today for the talents and knowledge I have—because they are gifts from you. I'm grateful for the pleasure I get from the skills I have.

O Giver of all gifts! Set my eyes on you today. Remind me when I am comparing myself to other people—to my own detriment or to theirs.

30
Trusting People

*To you [alone], O Lord, I lift up my soul; in you I
trust, O my God. Show me your ways . . . teach me
your paths; guide me . . . for you are God my Savior,
and my hope is in you all day long.*

Psalm 25:1, 4–5 [editor's note]

*I*t is natural to place your trust in people.

But how many times have you relied on someone to
help you, only to have them let you down? How many
times have you believed what someone is telling you
with all sincerity, only to find out later they "shaded"
the truth for some benefit of their own?

It is foolish to place the full weight of your soul—
that is, your *complete trust*—in people. When you do,
you set yourself up for disappointment, and eventually

133

you become closed and bitter. I am not telling you to distrust people and live in constant suspicion. But do you see what happens? When you rely totally on any man or woman, your trust is misplaced, and you wind up harming your own soul. . . .

Some Christians also fall into bitterness and disappointment when they put too much trust in the wisdom and guidance of other Christians, especially their spiritual leaders. When their counsel fails, they become angry or discouraged. "I listened to him, and his advice was bad. I never should have listened to anyone. I should have done what *I* thought was right. I'll never trust my life or my future to anyone . . . not even God."

And so the failure of some poor creature who is struggling to know God, too, ruins their soul.

The problem all along is this: *They trust in a creature more than they trust in God.*

If you seek Him with all your heart . . . if you tell Him you only want to fulfill His good will for your life . . . if you want to serve His purposes . . . He will guide you. *You can trust in that.*

I do not say that disappointments, setbacks, opposition, and even failure will not come to you.

These things are everyman's lot in life as long as we are in this fallen world. But when you know that your trust is in God, *and God alone*, you will not be cast down in soul.

Let your trust grow deeper in Him every day. He will lead you through every joy and success, all sorrow and loss. He will help you in every need—and through it all you will come to know His presence deep within you.

For He desires to give you what no man or woman can give—His very Spirit and life burning in your soul—so that nothing in this world can defeat or discourage you.

Father, I thank you that you want to do more than "guide" me or "help" me.

I thank you that you want to live in me!

Help me today to begin to trust you more fully—not to fulfill my will, but to fulfill your will through me.

Help me to trust you and you alone, before all others, so I am free and strong in spirit no matter what disappointments or challenges come today.

31

The Faults of Others

We urge you . . . encourage the timid, help the weak,
be patient with everyone. Make sure that nobody pays
back wrong for wrong, but . . . be kind to each other
and to everyone else.

1 Thessalonians 5:14–15

One of the most common pitfalls of the soul is to be distracted by the faults of other men and women.

By that I mean our tendency to see the flaws and mistakes of other people and *to use their imperfections as an excuse for our own.* "I'm not perfect," we say, "but no one is, and I am certainly not as bad as . . ."

Sometimes Christians use the faults of others to excuse themselves in another way. "Another Christian misused me," they say. Or, "I was so naïve. I thought I should be 'nice' and not push for what I wanted in that agreement. So he took advantage of me. See what being a Christian gets you?"

When we think this way, focused on the sins and flaws of others, we are still thinking like worldly people—measuring ourselves by the works of other people, thinking we are free from serving God and doing right because others do wrong.

You cannot help noticing the flaws in other people. But do not let them rule over you by dictating your attitudes and behavior. How do you escape this trap?

As I have been telling you all along, give your life every day to God. Remind your soul that He alone is the Lord and sovereign. Remind yourself that He has allowed your life to be full of flawed men, women, and children (people just as flawed as you). He allows this to teach you.

What is He teaching you?

First, to recognize the ways that others' faults affect you, how their mistakes make you angry, sad, or spiritually weak and full of excuses for your own behavior. Then He is teaching you to turn to Him for the strength to stop reacting as in the flesh and begin responding out of strength, a changed inner being, and in the Spirit of Christ.

He is using the flaws of others to grow the image of Christ in you.

Do you see it? This kind of growth in spirit is what God wants for us—not our token good works or our money. We can do or give all we want. But if our soul is not growing in Christ, all our outward religious activity means nothing.

Father, today help me not to put myself "above" others—noticing their flaws while I'm blind to my own—excusing my sins and failures because I'm "not as bad as they are." Help me to recognize that I am just the same in your eyes as all other men and women.

When the sin or mistake of another irritates me, open my eyes to the weakness in me that is responding with judgment and rejection. Instead, give me your response so I can react in grace, kindness, gentle guidance, and in your charity for all.

32

Dependence on "the World"

"Peace I leave with you; my peace I give you. I do not give to you [conditionally] as the world gives. Do not let your hearts be troubled. . . ."

John 14:27 [editor's note]

Are you easily upset when something you own is damaged or lost? Do you get offended or angry when people fail to do what you ask—or when they thoughtlessly ignore your needs?

When a situation doesn't work out as you'd hoped, are you dejected and dispirited?

These are all "signs" of the fact that you are too

dependent on the possessions, people, and circumstances of this life. A sign that your heart is too attached to these things and you are looking to them far too much for your security.

You see, in our need to be secure and know we are cared for, our heart tries to find its strength in what we can see—people, things, stable circumstances. We need to know our life and well-being are founded on something steady and unchanging. But in our fallen blindness, we try to build our security on what we can see with our physical eyes. And nothing that is created can offer the kind of stability the soul needs.

So we set our hearts on the things of this world, and as a result our affections are disordered. Our whole spirit is subject to constant disruption and shaking, as tragedy and loss strike all around and people come and go both making and breaking their promises.

Mostly, we are deceived by the *illusion* that things of this world are stable and secure—and by the illusion that they can offer us what we need for spiritual well-being. We crave the supposed "security" of wealth, the "worth" we will feel if someone else treats us right, the "satisfaction and happiness" we'll feel if we can get our hands on that certain possession we've been wanting.

But if these things had the power to give us want we want, why is it we still feel restless and unsteady when we get them in our grasp?

The man or woman who surrenders all their inner needs to God alone is the one who experiences abundance within. They experience rest from all the cravings that drive us to do more and have more. They experience the deep serenity that comes when you stop looking to vain and shallow things, and instead open up the center of your heart and allow God to dwell more fully in you.

I will not tell you it is easy—this battle to withdraw your heart from this world. Every one of us is a mixture of spiritual aspirations and affections and fleshly desires. And the voice of the world calls after us so piteously: "Think how sad and empty you'll be without these things you've wanted!"

But I can also tell you that it is by resisting the pull of the world and all it offers that brings the heart to rest—opening the way to the peace this world can never give.

*Father, I know I am blind to the "attachments"
I have to people and things—unaware of how much my
security, worth, and meaning are rooted in them.*

*I want to know what it is to "overcome" the world and to
have peace in my soul.*

*Now, in this moment, I ask you to fix my soul on your
greatness so I can know how good it is to stand strong and
confident—only in you.*

33
Habits

*"I will give [you] comfort . . . I will satisfy . . . and
my people will be filled. . . ."*

Jeremiah 31:13–14

I will be satisfied, [O God], with seeing your likeness.

Psalm 17:15 [editor's notes]

*M*any Christians find themselves stuck in habits
that are unhealthy for their bodies and displeasing to
God.

This is because we spend so much time—years for
some—seeking comfort for our souls in things that
pamper the flesh. We needed something that would

calm us, comfort us, restore a sense of inner peace, even if it was only temporary. We did not know how to turn to God, to still the demands of the upset soul and to allow Him to fill us with all that we needed.

And watch what happens when your particular "comfort" is denied you. You become testy and complaining. You can hardly stand to live with yourself—and other people truly cannot bear to live with you! Though we are grown people, we behave like babies.

It is God's goal that we become strong enough in spirit that the evil attacks of Satan and other people, and all the troubles of this life, become as nothing to us—falling to the ground with little effect as we become powerful and enduring in spirit. He wants our worth to be firmly based on the value He gives us, so that even when we are insulted to our face, our soul can say, "That's your opinion. I trust God alone to tell me what I'm worth." People who are growing strong in the Spirit of Christ can actually come to appreciate it when others speak evil of them—not because they like to be mistreated, but because it causes them to be more dependent on God for His word of approval. To live in His presence is their only happiness.

That is why I keep telling you: You need to escape this "need" to have earthly comforts. It is the reason I am taking such pains to tell you how to withdraw your heart and soul from dependence on the world rather than continuing to turn to it for comfort. It is a cold and brutal and capricious place at best, and nothing it offers can comfort you the way that drawing your inner life from God can.

Father, it's true, I am dependent on certain things: food and drink to comfort, new possessions to thrill me, hobbies and pastimes to distract me.

But I want to continue to grow and mature in spirit—to leave behind this babyish dependence on things to "pacify" me, and find stability and deep joy in your presence.

34
God Directs All Things

Better the little that the righteous have than the wealth of the wicked; for the power of the wicked will be broken, but the Lord upholds the righteous. The days of the blameless are known to the Lord, and their inheritance will endure forever.

Psalm 37:16–18

"*My* child," says the Lord. . . .

"You have begun to see that no matter how carefully you set up your life you cannot avoid struggle, pain, and sadness—not as long as you are in the world. But your struggles cause you to wonder about me. *Where is*

God when I need Him? Why doesn't He answer my prayers and take these troubles away from me?

"My child, it is not my will that you should find complete peace in a fallen world, where you live apart from me.

"It is not my will that you be free from temptation—because your pride would lead you to believe you are pure and holy in yourself, and you would not need to depend upon my mercy to make you clean, whole, and at peace in my forgiveness.

"It is not my will that you be free from opposition and setbacks—because your soul would find satisfaction right where you are, and you would not long to be with me, as I desire to be with you.

"It is my will that you learn how to view life from the right perspective. I want you to look at every struggle and temptation the world throws at you as a force motivating you to run to me. . . .

"I hear your complaints: *Why do some people have it so easy? I know people who are not Christians who have it much better than I do. They don't acknowledge or honor you as God—yet you let them enjoy a good life. They're happier than I am!*

"You are mistaken. Though you search the whole

world and look among those who appear the most well-off, you will never find anyone who is deeply happy or at peace in the depths of their being. Some hide their emptiness well. Some have taught themselves to focus so strongly on the things of this life that they keep themselves distracted from the gnawing in their soul.

"And still your soul resists the truth: *Yes, Lord . . . But at least they can afford worldly comforts to take their mind off their troubles. That seems like a good thing to me. If they can't have true inner happiness, at least they have pleasure and amusements.*

"I know that you believe this is a good thing, but you are wrong. Suddenly, all their worldly goods will be gone. The things that held their attention will vanish—like smoke dissipating in the air. Every one of them will pass from this life . . . and see all their treasures slipping from their fingers. Then they will be left to face the darkness . . . the empty gnawing that pulled at them all their lives. And they will face it alone, because all their lives they would not come to me.

"So you must see this: I direct all things that direct you to me. . . ."

O how short is this life! How empty are the

promises of this world! How senseless it is to spend your whole life filling yourself with temporary happiness . . . when you know that you are only in this world for a little while.

Father, keep speaking this word of reminder to my soul, because it's easy to become jealous of worldly people who have everything and seem to be happy without you. It's easy to think, "Why not live the way they do . . . and stop worrying about obeying God all the time?"

Remind me that I am only passing through this life . . . and one day this world will become as dust slipping through my fingers . . . and you and your eternal realm will become solid and real to me at last.

35

A Little "Sweetness"

Be strong in the grace [of the Lord]. . . . No one serving as a soldier gets involved in civilian affairs. . . . Reflect on what I am saying, for the Lord will give you insight. . . .

2 Timothy 2:1, 4, 7 [editor's note]

In your lifelong struggle to resist the allure of this world, you will always need to be on your guard.

For after a while, most men and women realize they will not have the fabulous wealth they dreamed about in their younger days. They realize they will not achieve everything they had hoped to achieve . . . and certainly very few will understand what great people they are!

And so it is not the desire for worldly greatness or

wealth that continues to hold many in bondage. It is a much smaller trap, really, so small as to go unnoticed. It is the quietest whisper of the world's voice, saying, "All right, then—if you are not going to have great things, then you deserve to have these small joys. You need a little sweetness to help you get through this tough life."

You see, the soul will always try to find its lasting shelter, its own heaven, somewhere apart from God. Even if it rests itself in the tiniest, most mundane little pleasures of earth.

Haven't you experienced this yourself? Don't you have some favorite food or drink? Or a special place? Or certain music you love? When you indulge yourself, you say, "This is heaven!"

So the little sweetnesses of life—and let us admit it, they are wonderful!—keep us from deeper union with God in Christ. We tell God, "Life is tough down here. Just let me have my little enjoyments. They aren't hurting you. . . ."

That is not the point. The fact is, something small and stupid may be keeping you from pressing on in spirit . . . until you find the utter sweetness that comes when you are abandoned to God—caught up in Him—

in the depths of your being. *That is ecstasy beyond anything man can describe.*

No, it is not that the sweetness of life's good things are bad in themselves ... only if they keep us from moving on to the higher, sweeter things.

This is why some Christians have learned to abstain from too much worldly pleasure. It is not that they are strange, not that they don't enjoy the good things of life like anyone else. But because they are like soldiers in training—avoiding the comforts of civilian life that would slowly make them out of shape—enjoying the power of an austere life that opens their soul to the burning joy of God's presence.

Father, show me today the small pleasures that I allow, which keep me from knowing greater delight in you.

36

"Imitate Jesus. . . ."

Your attitude should be the same as that of Christ Jesus: Who . . . made himself nothing . . . humbled himself and became obedient to death—even death on a cross! Therefore God exalted him. . . .

Philippians 2:5–9

"*My* child," says the Lord. . . .

"If you labor and strain to take yourself out from under my good and loving government over you, you will never know how I can empower you in the inner man.

"You will only know that power—my life and strength—in you when you come to the end of yourself. For it's then that you recognize how empty and powerless you are without me—then that you ask for strength, peace, love, and life that comes from beyond yourself. When you know you are poor in spirit, you are ready to rely on my grace. . . .

"This is when an amazing thing takes place. You recognize that every outward enemy can be defeated— not through your efforts, but by the power of my Spirit living through your surrendered spirit.

"There is no greater enemy to your soul than your *self*.

"And so I tell you, imitate my Son, Jesus . . . who came to show you how to live in the power that comes from emptying yourself so that I can fill you with my Spirit."

Father, I want to know you in your grace and power . . . and so I ask you to bring me to the depths of my weakness and inability.

Teach me what it means to lean upon you for my strength—to draw my purpose and life from you alone—and give me the courage to go beyond my fear, to give up control to you.

37
Await the Promises

The Lord is near to all who call on him. . . . He fulfills
the desires of those who fear [and wait upon] him. . . .
The Lord watches over all who love him. . . .

Psalm 145:18–20 [editor's note]

As I pursue God on this spiritual path of growth in Christ, I constantly remind myself of the fulfillment that awaits me. And the more I go on in life, the more I understand that His promises and comforts will only come to me fully when I am before Him—with Him forever.

Whatever I want by way of comfort and fulfillment—I know now I will never find it here on this earth. I know it will only be given to me in the life that is to come.

Or let's say that God allowed me to have all the comforts this world has to offer—let's say He allowed me to have every wish fulfilled (without being sinful, of course). I know now that the happiness I would experience would not last for long. In fact, as the thrill of having all my wishes fulfilled crumbled, I would no doubt experience such great disappointment and despair that the first rushes of happiness I'd felt would no longer seem worth it. . . .

And so I speak to my own soul when it is complaining, and tell it:

Wait. It will not harm you at all to wait a while longer. For the promise of God is certain as the dawn. He has given His Word—that you will find all your happiness in Him—and He will bring it to pass. You will experience such abundance of goodness in heaven that you will hardly be able to stand the happiness there. . . .

Then my soul becomes calm and patient within me. And to tell you the truth, I experience touches of a serene joy that is beyond words to describe, and must surely be a breath, a ray, of heaven coming into my soul.

Father, I know this earth is not heaven. I know that all your promises will not be fulfilled in my lifetime, but too often I demand that you give me what I think I need—now!

Father, you know my impatience. You know I cannot see beyond this minute, and how hard it is for me to wait. So, instead of answers, and more than promises, give me the joy of your real presence. Let all my needs be filled in the light of you.

38

"My child, trust in me."

I trust in your unfailing love. . . .

Psalm 13:5

I lift up my soul; in you I trust. . . .

Psalm 25:1

In God I trust; I will not be afraid.

Psalm 56:4

Those who trust in the Lord . . . cannot be shaken.

Psalm 125:1

"*M*y child," says the Lord, "You will only know true peace—that innocent freedom a child knows—when you relax and *trust me completely*.

"Trust me to do what I know is best for you. Trust me to decide what you need . . . for your comfort and happiness . . . for the strengthening of your faith . . . for your correction . . . to direct your steps and fulfill my purposes in you.

"You want to find the path that is good for you—but you spend all your time trying to determine the right plan for life. In your head you consider all the options, coming up with the course that will give you what you want, keep you free from harm, hedge you against loss. So you imagine. And you try to take on all my roles—as counselor, guide, friend, Father.

"Or else you let your heart take over. Then you are in real confusion! You feel strong emotions for this thing, and you are ready to commit your whole life, body and soul, to it. Then, in a few days, you wake to find your affections have grown cold. And then another interest, another "love," attracts you in a new direction . . . and off you go, chasing a new thing.

"And so you are in turmoil, your head at war with your heart. Your head trying to be cool and calculating.

Your heart running about from one love to the next. And even if, by chance, you should get control of these two, you are at best a blind guide. You cannot admit you do not know the best path to take. And you cannot see two minutes into the future. Nor can you see into the hearts and minds of people to whom you trust yourself.

"So you make wrong choices. And you are deceived by appearances and men's promises. . . . And then in your disappointment you say, " 'How did *God* let me go wrong?' "

O Lord, everything you say is true. I would be so much better off if I relaxed and trusted in your Spirit to guide me, every day, in the steps I need . . . just for that day. Better off if I trusted in your goodness, knowing that everything that happens to me is allowed by you for some good purpose—and that you will show me what that good is, if I let you.

It is true, indeed, that the man or woman who does not place all their trust in you—and you alone—walks through life on unsteady footing.

At this moment, Lord, my desire to be led by you is strong, though I know myself well enough to know I will not be this zealous about it tomorrow! My head and my heart will overrule my spirit again. So I beg you:

Take me at my word today. *Take hold of my hand . . . grab the reins of my soul . . . and do not let me go my own way tomorrow. Direct me, and do with me, according to your will. Remind me that there was this particular moment when I recognized you as Lord, sovereignly directing everything in my life, using all people and circumstances to accomplish your will. For tomorrow the eyes of the flesh may take over from the eyes of my soul, and I will be blind again, unable to see—or even sense—your hand leading me.*

For today I see clearly—you are only and always good. And because I am your child, when I trust in you, I can only walk in goodness. If it is your will to let me walk in "light," enjoying easy circumstances and many warm friendships— then, bless you! If it is your will to let me walk in "darkness," struggling with hardships without a friend in the world but you—I bless you for that, too. If you choose to send me many comforts in my life, for my body and my soul—well, of course, I will bless you for that! But if you send not one person to console me—even for that, I bless you.

I know this: Only by trusting you . . . only by keeping the eyes of my soul fixed on you . . . can I overcome the devil, the flesh, and the world . . . and know the fire of your presence within me.

"My child," says the Lord, "This is the attitude you must keep at all times. For I will truly guide you through all things . . . and there is nothing you will experience in life that is beyond my control.

"Keep your eyes on me then—whether you are in very hard circumstances or in a time of happiness, whether you have little or a lot, whether life tastes bitter or sweet."

Father—keep me.

39

Accept Me, Father

Blessed be the God and Father of our Lord Jesus Christ. . . . He hath chosen us . . . [and] made us accepted in the beloved.

Ephesians 1:3–4, 6 *KJV*

Can you see now that everything in heaven and earth belongs to the Lord?

Do you understand that nothing is beyond His reach? No circumstance is too great for Him to take charge of?

There is no situation, provision, or person He cannot command and send to your aid, if that is what He wills. You are surrounded by Him, behind and before, above and below—surrounded by the One who is Love itself. Is that not enough to make you cast all your care upon Him? Doesn't it make your heart want to pledge complete allegiance to Him, so that you say, "I trust you, great Father, more than anything or anyone in my life!"

Lord, I give myself to you freely. I offer all of me to you . . . so that from this moment until I step into eternity I am living in your presence.

Lord, I have no other motive than this: I want to live simply as your child, receiving directly from your hand whatever you will give me from day to day . . . hour to hour. Instead of pressing you to serve me and my purposes, I will serve you, and constant praise for your goodness will be on my lips.

Accept me, Father. I offer myself to you today, with the holy angels as witnesses. Restore me to the company of your presence and the strength of your outpouring grace, which was lost at the Fall.

In this moment, I sense you coming near to me, Father, wrapping me in your arms of love, taking me to your heart . . . with the kiss of forgiveness . . . and peace.

I give my life to you.

40
Journey's End

How lovely is your dwelling place,
O Lord Almighty! My soul yearns, even faints,
for the courts of the Lord; my heart and my flesh
cry out for the living God.

———

Psalm 84:1–2

Shout with joy to God. . . .
Sing the glory of his name. . . . Say to God,
"How awesome are your deeds! So great is your power
that your enemies cringe before you.
All the earth bows down to you. . . ."

———

Psalm 66:1–4

You, Lord God, are the most high.

You are the most good . . . the most mighty, most capable of giving all I need. You are sweetest in kindness and in correction. You are most fierce in your love—so noble and selfless.

From within you come the most intense rays of glory—all the truth, beauty, love, holiness that has ever shone! My soul is stabbed with joy and wonder when I look into your brightness.

In you all goodness fits together—everything good that ever has been or ever can be.

Father, you may give me many things in my life—things I desire, things that surprise and delight me. But whatever you give me besides yourself will be small in comparison. Your gifts will make my heart glad for a time, but that happiness will fade. It will not be enough to give me the life from within, which I need to sustain me through the battles of this life . . . to keep me strong on this long journey.

What is it I need?

Above all created things, my heart needs to find its home and resting-place in you.

O Lord!—Lover of my soul, Ruler of all things! I ask that you give me the wings of freedom—freedom to rise above all the things of this life that keep me from flying to your side, where I can rest myself in you.

You alone are my victory in every battle. . . . You are every journey's end. . . .

Father—Light and Beauty of everlasting glory! Come quickly when I call, as I make my way through the struggles and joys of this life.

Today, and every day, I will find the strength and life of my soul eternally in you!